Original title:
Life's Journey: Taking the Scenic Route

Copyright © 2025 Creative Arts Management OÜ
All rights reserved.

Author: Atticus Thornton
ISBN HARDBACK: 978-1-80566-223-5
ISBN PAPERBACK: 978-1-80566-518-2

The Allure of Unknown Destinations

Packed my bag with snacks and dreams,
Took a left turn, or so it seems.
Lost my way but found a cat,
He led me home, imagine that!

Maps are guides, but who needs those?
Chasing ice cream in purple clothes.
Every twist, an adventure's call,
I'll get there eventually, after all!

The Dance of Time and Space

Tick-tock clocks have lost their beat,
As I traipse down the quirky street.
I step on cracks, dance with glee,
Maybe I'll trip, who cares, not me!

Time bends like a rubber band,
I just waved at a marching band.
Lost an hour, found a friend,
And all it took was a twisty bend!

Moments Between the Milestones

Milestones come and milestones go,
But what about the bites of dough?
I pause to snack, oh what a thrill,
Savoring life's sweet cupcake spill.

Between the steps, I twirl and cheer,
Life's a circus, full of cheer!
I might fall down, but that's okay,
I'll just laugh and eat more hay!

The Pathway of Possibilities

With every fork, a choice I make,
Should I swim or bake a cake?
Paths diverge like silly straws,
I take the one with laughter's cause.

Pros and cons; I'll toss a coin,
Flip it hard, my fate's the point.
Down the trail of whimsical fun,
I find the joy; I've already won!

Byways of the Heart

I took a turn too quick one day,
My GPS still in dismay.
I ended up at a cow parade,
Their mooing led me to a charade.

With every twist and every bend,
New friends found around the bend.
A goat gave me directions clear,
So I laughed and shed a tear.

The Road Unfolds

The map I had was quite a joke,
Told me to find the nearest smoke.
Instead, I found a lollipop stand,
Where sprinkles did dance like a marching band.

The shortcuts never seem quite right,
But candy can make your day feel bright.
I left feeling a little round,
With sugar high all over town.

Memories in the Footprints

Each step I take can bring a laugh,
Especially when I trip on grass.
My footprints tell tales of the clumsy way,
With scribbles of laughter and wild ballet.

A puddle splashes, oh, what a sight!
A spontaneous dance in the moonlight.
Friends join in and cheer me on,
Together we're silly until the dawn.

A Canvas of Curves

Winding roads like a painter's brush,
Create a scene that makes hearts rush.
With funky signs and a crooked tree,
I find my muse, embracing glee.

The journey's not straight, it's a wild ride,
With laughter and snacks as my guide.
So here I roam, carefree and free,
In a world where smiles are meant to be.

Journeys Between the Lines

We set out with a plan in mind,
But pit stops leave our map behind.
With snacks and laughter, we roam far,
GPS? Nah, we follow the stars.

Julie's got the snacks, Tom drives the car,
We take the wrong exit, oh, that's bizarre!
Every turn's a tale, the wrong way's the best,
We'll never win awards, but we'll ace the jest.

Dreamscapes on the Horizon

There's a billboard for a giant shoe,
We stop to snap a pic or two.
Pigeon on the hood, looking like a king,
Who knew that travel could be this bling?

We dream of beaches, we find a field,
With cows as our guides, so surreal!
With each glance at cows, we burst into glee,
What great companions for a road trip spree!

The Roots Beneath the Journey

Map's upside down, we're lost in a grove,
But capers we make—oh, how we drove!
A squirrel gives us directions with a wave,
Who knew that nature could be this brave?

We stop for ice cream, melt in the sun,
While the cone drips—oh, it's all in good fun!
We end up with laughter, and sticky shoes,
Making memories in the world's biggest zoo!

Stories in Every Station

At the station, a man sells hot dogs and dreams,
We barter our stories, or so it seems.
A toddler giggles, rides the train with flair,
Life's simple moments, we all want our share.

With viewfinders out, we spot funny sights,
A cat in a hat, in the morning light!
Each station we hit, there's a tale to tell,
The art of the journey? We do it quite well!

Journeys Through the Heart's Landscape

Each step feels like a dance,
With two left feet, I prance.
The map's upside down, oh dear,
But I'll follow the laughter here.

Every turn is quite a twist,
I swear the GPS is missed.
Found a cow that stole my hat,
Now that's how the story's spat!

Lost my way in a buttercup,
And my coffee's in a teacup.
With every bump, I ride the wave,
Who knew adventures could be brave?

So here's to paths that veer and stray,
With muddy shoes and joy at play.
We're all just sketches in the sand,
Winding paths made by chance's hand.

Where the Wildflowers Grow

In fields of daisies, I take a chat,
With a squirrel who thinks he's cool as that.
He talks about nuts and life's great stew,
I nod and laugh, as squirrels do.

Oh look, a bloom that's tall and proud,
It's wearing pollen like a crown, how loud!
I try to pose for a selfie shot,
But a bee photobombs, so never mind that plot.

The breeze likes to tease my hair just right,
While ants are on a tiny flight.
I trip over roots, what a graceful fall,
Nature laughs, oh yes, it knows it all.

I gather blooms for a wild bouquet,
And watch the clouds drift and sway.
With petals bright, I feel alive—
In this silly dance, I truly thrive.

Curves of Adventure

Around the bend, I take a leap,
On this bumpy road, I laugh and weep.
With every twist, I spin like a top,
Who knew a nap in the car would stop?

The sign says 'Detour,' I squeal with glee,
Like a kid who spots a lurid spree.
I chase the butterflies, miss the turns,
Oh, look! A flower shop that burns!

I sidestep puddles, a wet waltz I do,
Sprinkling laughter in morning dew.
Chased by a goat—what a wild scene,
Should've packed more than just sunscreen!

Finally, I stumble on a quaint little place,
With quirky signs and a smiling face.
Adventure's curve is my favorite role,
With stories to sprinkle and a happy soul.

Sunsets and Serendipity

Chasing sunsets, colors collide,
A funny duck quacks, says let's glide!
I fumble with my camera's snap,
Oops! I caught my finger in the lap.

The sky blushes in peach and gold,
While I juggle ice cream, so bold.
A swirl drips down and stains my shirt,
But laughter floats, it won't even hurt.

A picnic blanket flies like a kite,
As we chase our grapes in pure delight.
The ants are dancing at our feet,
What a spot for this delicious treat!

So here's to days where mischief reigns,
Sunny smiles wash away the pains.
With every sunset, a story spins,
In this tale of joy, everyone wins!

Constellations of Experience

In a car with snacks piled high,
We took the road, you and I.
Stopping to smell the wildflowers,
Counting cows for hours and hours.

Maps upside down, a glorious sight,
Turned left when we should've gone right.
Each bump and turn a laughter spree,
You swore we were lost, but look, we're free!

The GPS now looks so confused,
"Recalculating," it loudly accused.
Yet unfolding tales in every mile,
We chuckled as we mismanaged style.

Through the fields of questionable fate,
We held on tight, while debating fate.
Perhaps wrong turns are just right moves,
In this dance where the road grooves.

The Poetry of Passing Places

A diner made of mustard and dreams,
Where the coffee flows and laughter beams.
The waitress must be part-time sage,
With wisdom served on a side of rage.

In towns where the clocks forget to tick,
We wander through with our usual tricks.
Every corner hides a tale untold,
In the colors of the stories bold.

In the bookstore with ten cats on the floor,
We found old maps and a dusty lore.
Each step a giggle, each shelf a cheer,
Grabbing a moment, not a career.

As sunset paints the skies in gold,
We weave our path, brave and bold.
So here's to stops along the way,
In passing places, we learn to play.

Open Windows and Open Hearts

With windows down and music loud,
We danced like fools, oh-so-proud.
The world rushed by, like a fleeting ghost,
Belting tunes, we sang the loudest boast.

Spontaneous stops at a roadside stand,
Where watermelon juice is simply grand.
The sticky sweetness dripped from our chins,
Laughter shared, where the fun begins.

We flirted with strangers, shared silly dreams,
Invented tales that burst at the seams.
Each open heart, like a star in the night,
Leading us onward, onward, to delight.

Through the trees, where the wild things play,
We drove 'til dusk chased the day away.
With every giggle and every laugh,
The windows wide, creating our path.

Shadows of Doubt and Light

In the headlights, shadows appeared,
We laughed them off, what we revered.
With every twist, we questioned our way,
But found some gold at the end of the fray.

Did you see that sign? It read 'To Nowhere'!
We stopped for selfies, with no single care.
With awkward grins and poses far too fake,
Captured memories, that's the only take!

The road may twist with doubts and sighs,
Yet we laughed as the miles piled high.
In shadows cast by what we don't know,
We'll dance in the light, just watching it glow.

So here's to the murky paths we tread,
To tales we tell, and a life well-spread.
With shadows dancing and laughter so light,
We'll ride together 'til the morning bright.

Footprints in the Mist

In morning fog, I step so light,
My shoes get lost, what a funny sight!
Each print a tale in swirling haze,
Did I just walk through yesterday's maze?

A squirrel laughs at my floundering pace,
While I try to find my missing space.
With every stumble, I cackle loud,
The mist just giggles, teasing the crowd.

As I trip over a wayward twig,
I swear it winked, now that's too big!
Nature plays tricks, oh such a tease,
Making my journey a comedy piece.

Through blurry paths, I wander free,
Chasing shadows that laugh with glee.
With footprints fading, I dance in bliss,
Leave it to fog to conjure this twist!

Seasons of Discovery

In spring I stumble on blooming cheer,
A bee buzzes by, oh dear, oh dear!
I duck and weave like a dizzy hen,
Chasing butterflies with wild-eyed zen.

Summer rolls in with a sunburned grin,
Ice cream drips down, oh where to begin?
I chase the cone as it slips from my hand,
A sticky mess, isn't life just grand?

Autumn leaves swirl, I try to catch one,
They laugh and tease, oh this is such fun!
I trip and tumble, hear the crisp snap,
Life's a dance, take a silly lap!

Winter arrives with a frosty chill,
I slip on ice, oh what a thrill!
Sledding down hills, I laugh with a hoot,
Embracing the chaos, this life's a hoot!

The Harmony of Footsteps

Each step I take, a toe-tapping beat,
I'm a marching band with two left feet.
The rhythm's off, but who even cares?
I groove through puddles with style that flares.

In sync with the birds who laugh in the trees,
They chirp my tune, with all manners of ease.
But watch out now, I'm a clumsy fool,
Twisting and turning in this wacky duel.

Over rocks and roots, I dance and sway,
My shadow giggles, leading the way.
With every misstep, a chuckle erupts,
As the melody of life happily interrupts.

So join my parade, don't be shy,
Let's waddle and wobble, you and I!
For in this folly, we find our song,
A symphony of laughter, where we belong!

Colors of a Meandering Path

Down the winding path where colors collide,
I stumble on green, then blue, then wide.
Roses on my left, daisies on my right,
Can't decide which blooms spark my delight.

A rainbow spills across my eyesight,
I slip in a puddle, what a comical fright!
Each splash sends laughter into the air,
The critters join in, without a care.

Through a groovy pond with frogs on parade,
I join in their chorus, quite unafraid.
Croaking like pros, what a bizarre sound,
In this painted land, joy knows no bound.

So follow the path where colors unite,
With giggles and blunders, take flight!
Every turn a hue, every step a cheer,
A canvas of chaos, vibrant and dear!

The Art of Wandering

I packed a bag with snacks galore,
But ended up at a llama store.
They stared at me with puzzled eyes,
Guess they don't sell glitter ties.

I took a turn, oh, what a sight,
Found a tree that looked just right.
Turns out it was a giant stump,
Gave my dreams a little bump.

A map in hand, I felt so wise,
Yet ended up where pizza flies.
A slice as big as my delight,
Might just be my next flight.

So here I am, lost in the fun,
Wandering where I can't outrun.
I'll chase the clouds or stop for tea,
In this merry place, I'm wild and free.

Kaleidoscope of Experiences

Through rainbows bright and puddles deep,
I jumped and splashed, lost in a leap.
Each twist of fate, a silly game,
The ducks now quack my middle name.

A biker passed, then hit a bump,
His fancy seat, a perfect slump.
We laughed so hard the sky turned blue,
And life danced on in every hue.

I tried to jog, but tripped on shoes,
Found myself with dancing blues.
A squirrel laughed, it joined the beat,
We wiggled on, still tasting sweet.

The world spins round, it twirls and bends,
With every turn, a new surprise blends.
I gather moments like colorful beads,
In this wild ride, laughter leads.

Sunlit Steps Towards Tomorrow

I wore my hat, it looked quite grand,
But then it flew from my own hand.
Chased it down, in fits of glee,
Only to find a laughing bee.

With sunlit steps I made my way,
Each twist and turn brought pure cliché.
I met a cat who wore a tie,
We shared a laugh and wondered why.

Sandwiches tossed in the air,
I caught one, it smelled of flair.
But onward I thought, what a joy,
I opted for a rubber toy.

Tomorrow's just a wink away,
With antics bright and plans at play.
I'll skip along with no real map,
For every detour's a funny gap.

Into the Unknown: A Traveler's Tale

I packed my map, or so I thought,
But what I grabbed was just a rot.
A treasure map to nowhere grand,
  Led me straight to a jolly band.

They sang of ships that sail in soup,
Invited me to be part of the troupe.
I danced with spoons, twirled with glee,
Who knew spoons could dance with me?

A pigeon cooed, it shared its snack,
We feasted more, no looking back.
Where's the end? I've lost my way,
  Maybe tomorrow—it's okay!

So here I am, in laughter's sway,
Tomorrow's troubles, I'll delay.
Into the unknown, come what may,
  I'll find the fun in each display.

Roadside Revelations

There's a sign for the world's largest ball,
But I found it was nothing at all.
In a diner, I ordered a slice,
And found it was mostly just ice!

A cow took a selfie, oh what a sight,
It posed with a grin, what a pure delight!
We laughed as it mooed, quite out of tune,
I wished I could join its bovine commune.

Winding roads lead to nowhere fast,
But hey, let's make memories that last!
With donuts and coffee, we're feeling alive,
Driving like squirrels, oh how we thrive!

Each wrong turn a tale to regale,
From flat tires to fish that don't bail.
With maps that have kissed an old tree,
I wonder if we'll find Utopia, or a flea?

Embracing the Dusty Trails

On a path with no GPS in sight,
We took a left turn that felt just right.
A rusted-out truck became our cafe,
With sandwiches made in a strange ballet!

The dust of the road danced up like a sprite,
Hitchhikers had signs, a peculiar sight.
One read 'free hugs', the other 'good vibes',
We laughed so hard, we lost all our scribes!

The wind told us stories of travelers past,
Who probably wondered, 'Am I going too fast?'
We embraced the quirks of our own little lane,
As laughter echoed through sunshine and rain.

With hiccups and giggles, we ventured ahead,
Finding fortune in fries instead of bread.
In this dusty jaunt, we found our own bliss,
Fuelled by chuckles and a spontaneous kiss!

The Compass of Curiosity

Who needs directions when fun's in the air?
With a compass that spins, we've abandoned despair.
Left, right, or straight—wherever it leads,
We'll follow our noses, just like curious breeds!

A store selling rubber chickens caught my eye,
And a man wearing flip-flops and a pink tie.
We couldn't resist; we joined the parade,
Where laughter and chaos were wonderfully laid!

Chasing butterflies, pretending to fly,
We plotted our course beneath the clear sky.
With a snack of some cookies and fizzy drinks,
Why worry about time when the heart truly shrinks?

As the sunset painted the world bright and bold,
We promised to treasure this moment we stole.
Curiosity's compass spun wildly with glee,
Leading us home, hand in hand, you and me!

Faded Signs and Fresh Beginnings

Faded signs whisper secrets of yore,
Like 'turn back now' but we want more!
With paint peeling off from sunlight's caress,
We're steered by adventures, I must confess!

'World's best tea' shared with a goat,
Who stole my sandwich, what a sneaky note!
He chewed with finesse, giving me a wink,
I wondered if goats like playing with ink?

Rivers of laughter flow down the lane,
While a cat on a skateboard avoids all the rain.
Faded maps lie scattered in the back,
But fresh smiles lead us, never off track.

With every bump, our spirits ignite,
As missteps become the heart of the night.
Faded signs cannot halt our quest,
For fresh beginnings are always the best!

Masquerade of the Open Air

In a hat too big, I prance around,
With mismatched socks on the merry ground.
The clouds all giggle, the sun gives a wink,
As I trip on my laces, not quite in sync.

I dance with the breeze, twirling my chin,
While squirrels debate where my snacks have been.
A butterfly lands, my hat is a stage,
And all of the flowers clap with great rage.

With every step, I find a new route,
A puddle becomes a pond, watch me hoot!
The map is a puzzle, the roads are a jest,
In this funny charade, I'm truly the best.

So if you see me, just join in the fun,
We'll hop over rainbows and laugh 'til we run.
With giggles and blunders, let's make our own scene,
In this masquerade, where laughter is keen.

The Fabric of Wandering Souls

In the patchwork of life, I sew with delight,
Stitching together both day and the night.
Each thread tells a tale, a mishap, a laugh,
A button that pops, oh, what a craft!

As I wander through fields, my pockets are stuffed,
With treasures I found, and snacks that I guffed.
The compass is broken, it points to a grin,
As the fabric of fate pulls the mischief within.

With a needle of chaos and yarn made of dreams,
I'll patch up the moments, split at the seams.
A weaving of wonders, both silly and true,
In the quilt of existence, I'm stitching with you.

So let's grab our needles, let's make quite a mess,
In the fabric of wandering, we'll never compress.
Each blunder a gem, a colorful thread,
In this tapestry vibrant, forever widespread.

Treadlight Among the Tall Trees

In the woods I tiptoe, my shoes are a joke,
Each crack of a twig makes the tall trees poke.
I dangle like vines, all floppy and spry,
With squirrels as my jesters, oh my, oh my!

The branches chuckle, they tickle my nose,
While I concoct plans for a woodland show.
A stage made of leaves and a crowd full of ants,
As I tumble and stumble, they all do their dance.

A deer rolled its eyes, a raccoon gave a huff,
"Just treadlight," they said, "or we'll call your bluff."
But laughter's my armor, my giggles, they soar,
In this forest of whimsy, where fun's at the core.

So let's skitter and scatter, let the tall trees sway,
In this playground of green, we'll forever play.
With whispers of nature, we'll skip with delight,
As we treadlight and free in the soft, golden light.

Nature's Melodies and Midnight Stars

In the woods, I heard a tune,
A chipmunk's dance, beneath the moon.
Birds were harmonizing sweet,
With crickets playing bass to their beat.

I tried to sing but got it wrong,
A frog joined in, and we were strong.
The owls hooted, what a show!
I swear we launched a wild karaoke flow!

Stars were twinkling like they had flair,
They seemed to giggle at our affair.
In nature's band, we felt so grand,
Making melodies in this wild land.

But as the sun began to rise,
We all turned quiet and said goodbyes.
The woods were free, a stage so vast,
With nature's tunes, we had a blast!

The Map of the Mind

I rolled out maps, both old and new,
To chart a course, with coffee too.
Each route I took, went in a twist,
I lost my way, oh how I missed!

Thoughts led me here, thoughts led me there,
Got stuck in traffic on a wild hare.
I took a detour through a giant's shoe,
And stumbled upon a carnival zoo!

The map flipped over, I held it tight,
Got caught in dreams of a giant kite.
With every path, I lost my way,
Yet somehow, I enjoyed my play!

So here I am, no need for haste,
A winding trip can't go to waste.
The mind's a maze, and I hold the key,
Let's laugh and wander, just you and me!

Searching for Shelters

In the rain, I sought a place,
With ducks as my companions, what a chase!
I found a tree, sturdy and wide,
Joined by squirrels, too, on the side.

To their chatter, I shared my woes,
They chirped and laughed, in comic prose.
A raccoon peeked out from behind the bark,
Said, "Join my party! Let's light a spark!"

We built a camp, with leaves and glee,
A shelter made, just you and me.
With snacks of acorns, we dined divine,
In our little haunt, we felt just fine.

As the storm cleared, we waved goodbye,
My furry friends began to fly.
With giggles echoing all around,
We found our shelter, safe and sound!

Across the Horizon: A Tapestry of Paths

With every sunset, a new route calls,
I trip on laughter as the daylight falls.
The horizon stretches, a painted hue,
I race the shadows beneath the blue.

I met a snail who shared his dream,
To zoom through fields at the speed of cream.
He took a breath and off he went,
A slow-motion hero, more than I'd meant!

A bird swooped low, introduced its flight,
"Meet me at dusk!" It chirped with delight.
Together we soared over hills and streams,
Painting horizons with whimsical dreams.

As I journeyed on, the stars winked bright,
Every turn filled with joy and slight fright.
Across all paths, with laughter embraced,
A tapestry woven, no moment misplaced.

Memories Written on the Wind

I set my course for adventure's flair,
With snacks in hand and messy hair.
The GPS said, 'Turn right at the tree,'
But I found myself near a burnt-out BBQ spree.

A raccoon crossed my path with a strut,
I offered a donut, he said, 'What a glut!'
We chuckled together, both lost in the mist,
And off I went, adding to my twist.

When clouds gathered, I braced for the rain,
A car splashed me, oh what a pain!
Yet I turned it to giggles, soaked to the bone,
This wild and silly ride felt like home.

So here's to the travels that never go planned,
With friends like raccoons, who need a map in hand?
For memories are made, as winds dance and sing,
In every odd stop, joy is the thing.

The Unexpected Turn

I took a wrong turn, but where to begin?
Found myself at a goat yoga spin.
The goats did their poses, and I tried too,
But I fell over – mud all over my shoe!

Next, I stumbled upon a strange little fair,
With folks in costumes, I stopped to stare.
A juggler dropped balls right into my hat,
I laughed till I cried—how's that for a spat?

The map said to go to the café for a treat,
But I ended up at a hot dog retreat.
With toppings so wild, there's no way to plan,
A pickle and jelly? Sure, just for the 'gram!

With every turn taken, a smile did bloom,
Life's little mishaps dispel every gloom.
So here's to the paths that twist and that swerve,
With wacky adventures, we always reserve.

Echoes of Laughter Along the Way

In search of the best ice cream shop, I roamed,
And ended up where a llama was combed.
With each wink and nudge, my heart took flight,
We shared a cone, oh, what a sight!

At times I get lost, but it's part of the game,
As I meet quirky souls in the midst of the fame.
A mime stole my fries with a sly little grin,
And like a good sport, I let the fun begin!

Oh, the lessons learned are not on the map,
But in ice cream spills and a friendly clap.
Humor's the ticket, to take in the scene,
From clumsy dance moves to llamas so keen.

So raise a cone high to the laugh-out-loud days,
For joy's in the moments, in all of their ways.
The echoes of laughter, from here to afar,
Are the stories we weave—our true guiding star.

Vistas of the Heart

On a road with a view, I stopped with a grin,
To check out the landscape and let laughter in.
A squirrel ran by, doing acrobat tricks,
As I laughed so hard, I nearly got sick!

With grand scenic vistas, I felt quite the muse,
Until I stepped back and stood on my shoes.
A tree branch poked out, I yelped with a start,
But the woodland critters invited me to art.

A bear in a hat offered me tea,
'It's chamomile, dear, it's excellent see!'
Together we painted, with paws and my hands,
In the gallery of nature, our fun-making stands.

So I raise my toast to the beauty of chance,
With unexpected moments, there's always a dance.
In vistas so vast, the heart finds its glee,
In the quirks of the journey, just be wild and free.

On the Edge of Tomorrow

Time's a caffeine fiend, racing past,
Got coffee stains on my future cast.
I trip on dreams, I juggle my fears,
Then slip on a banana, as laughter nears.

With calendars burning, I throw out plans,
And dance like a chicken while life just scans.
On streets paved with puddles, I splash and twirl,
This is how chaos makes my head whirl.

Caught in the traffic of daily grind,
But I'm the clown who's joyfully blind.
I skipped down the road with mismatched socks,
To chase after sunlight and tickle the clocks.

So here's to the madness, the slips and the slides,
In this shimmering fun-house, where whimsy abides.
Tomorrow's just waiting, with glitter and glee,
As I stumble through life, eternally free!

Canvas of Unwritten Stories

With a paintbrush of hopes and a palette of dreams,
I color outside lines, or so it seems.
Each splash a misstep, each stroke a surprise,
Creating a masterpiece right before my eyes.

From doodles in my head to paint spills on the floor,
Popcorn in my pockets, who could want more?
I'll frame my mishaps and hang them up high,
In a gallery showcasing my freakshow sky.

With every blank page, I whisper out loud,
Turn failures to giggles and frowns to a crowd.
I'm scribbling nonsense, waltzing with fate,
Filling my canvas with chaos and plate.

So grab your own colors, let laughter erupt,
We'll splash on the canvas and never give up.
Every line tells a tale, every flaw a delight,
In this gallery of life, let's paint it bright!

Nature's Interludes

Gardens of giggles sprout from the cracks,
Nature humorously plays all the pranks.
Bees buzzing jokes as they flit to and fro,
While flowers gossip, in their own little show.

Mountains are chuckling, hills roll in glee,
As squirrels are the comedians, setting us free.
A leaf takes a tumble, doing flips in the air,
Nature's up to something without a care.

Rivers are laughing, their giggle's a flow,
With stones that sing ballads to poetic woe.
In this outdoor theater, the world takes its cue,
As trees dance the cha-cha with a bright, leafy crew.

So let's wander the wild, with marbles to spare,
Chasing the whimsy of cool, gentle air.
Amidst all the nature, let silly hearts start,
Collecting the moments that tickle the heart!

Chasing Shadows and Light

On sunny days, shadows play tag,
While I trip on my feet, let the light brag.
Chasing reflections that wobble and sway,
I dance with my shadow in the silliest way.

In the dusk, all my worries delude,
As shadows grow long, my path gets renewed.
With a hop and a skip, I tumble with glee,
My shadow's my buddy, it's just you and me.

Gliding through laughter, let giggles ignite,
The shadows and sunshine make everything bright.
I run with abandon, scream at the sky,
Why worry 'bout darkness? Just give it a try!

Chasing the echoes of twilight's embrace,
Where shadows get funny, and light leaves a trace.
So on this wild ride, let's swirl through the night,
Together we'll frolic, chasing joy and delight!

Sights Beyond the Map

I took a turn, I can't recall,
And found a sign for a giant mall.
They've got a ride that goes uphill,
With snacks in hand, oh what a thrill!

I thought I'd see some mountains high,
Instead I met a grumpy guy.
He sold me dreams of ice cream hills,
But all I got was empty swills.

My GPS lost its sense of humor,
Tried to reroute me to a rumor.
"Recalibrating," it always cried,
Meanwhile, I just enjoyed the ride!

With every twist, I laugh and scoff,
Each wrong turn, a chuckle soft.
So here's to paths unplanned, beware,
You find the best sights hanging there!

Gentle Breezes and New Beginnings

A gentle breeze, a butterfly,
I waved and thought, 'Oh me, oh my!'
With every flap, they fluttered near,
I wondered if they couldn't steer.

I met a cat who claimed to know,
The shortcuts through the weeds and snow.
He led me on quite the chase,
Ended up just lost in space!

A couple of ducks quacked out a tune,
Partied hard under the harvest moon.
I picked a spot to dance and sing,
Except I tripped and lost my bling!

But through the giggles and the slips,
I learned that joy's in all the flips.
So if you stumble, laugh it loud,
Join the merry, dancing crowd!

Echoes of the Past

Walking through a field of shoes,
Each one holds a tale to choose.
A pair of flip-flops once so bright,
Tells of beach days and late-night bites.

I stumbled on a skateboard's track,
That sparked memories of an old snack.
I used to ride like I was cool,
'Til one last tree became my rule!

A yo-yo danced back in my mind,
With every loop, a laugh I find.
Those awkward days of youth we see,
Just shaped the person that's still me!

So if you hear the past's embrace,
Just grin and dance, don't lose your pace.
For every remember is like a cheer,
Echoing fun, bringing joy near!

Lost and Found in the Wilderness

Trekking through the woods alone,
I found a bear with a funny tone.
He said, "You lost? I've got some snacks!"
Just my luck, he had some hacks!

We shared some berries, got a bit washed,
By a river that bubbled and splashed.
He told me tales of forest fame,
And how to avoid a messy game!

A rabbit hopped with a sassy flick,
Challenged me to a very quick trick.
I tried to leap, but fell right down,
And the rabbit laughed, I lost my crown!

But then I learned, with each new fall,
Adventure's better when shared by all.
So here's to laughter in the wild,
Where every mishap feels like a child.

Harmony in the Unexpected

In a world where plans go awry,
I once tried to bake, oh my!
The cake took a flop, it flew like a bird,
Now I'm known as the pastry nerd.

Maps in my pocket, GPS on the fritz,
Got lost in a town where they spoke in bits.
But the local diner served pie with a grin,
And I chatted with folks about where they had been.

With wrong turns behind every hairpin bend,
I found a new world to laugh and mend.
Each detour a treasure, each stumble a gem,
Life's punchlines are waiting, so let's hit 'em again.

So here's to the missteps, the odd little ways,
Where laughter erupts and spontaneity plays.
Embrace the bizarre, let joy take the reins,
In the waltz of existence, it's all in the gains.

Tides of Change and Wonder

Oh, I thought I could surf, but what a delight!
Rolling in waves that gave quite a fright.
I landed in seaweed, made friends with a crab,
He winked with a claw, could've sworn he was fab.

With a suitcase of dreams, I hopped on a train,
Except it was broken, and I felt pretty vain.
The conductor just laughed, served us popcorn for free,
We danced in the aisles, just the train and me.

Setting sail on a ship, the map upside down,
The compass went crazy, spun round like a clown.
Yet with each wave crash, I grinned through the mess,
For a wrong turn may lead to a fabulous quest.

So here's to the breeze that pushes us wide,
And the wacky surprises we find on the ride.
With sun in our faces, and laughter the sound,
We'll surf every wave till the shore comes around.

The Surrounding Silence

In the forest, I wandered, seeking some peace,
But a squirrel chittered loudly, 'Oh, what a tease!'
He scolded my path and threw down some nuts,
I laughed at his wrath, with all of his guts.

Tried to meditate while perched on a rock,
But a raccoon joined in, thought it fun to knock.
He batted my thoughts like a ball on a spree,
And serenity crumbled, just him and just me.

The silence I sought turned a comedy show,
With a parade of antics, I couldn't say no.
Each critter had tales that made my heart sing,
In their chatter and play, I found bliss in the spring.

So here's to the moments we find so absurd,
When nature's a jester, not a silent bird.
Embrace all the chaos, let laughter collide,
In the symphony of silliness, let joy be your guide.

A Journey of Many Colors

Packed my bags for a trip, thought I'd keep it neat,
But the socks snuck out, trapped beneath my seat.
Now every shoe's a shade of bizarre,
With patterns so wild, I'm a walking art star.

Took a road full of bumps with snacks in the back,
My soda exploded—oh, what a whack!
The map got a tear from a fast-flying chip,
And I wound up straying from the main road trip.

At a carnival stop, I tried my luck there,
With a mustached man who had lavender hair.
He won me a prize, a cat in a hat,
Add that to my collection of brightly clad brats.

So here's to the hues that bring laughter and cheer,
To the wacky adventures that bring memories near.
Each twist and each turn holds a splash of delight,
In this colorful life, let your laughter take flight.

Traces of Time on the Road

With every twist and every turn,
We find out what we have to learn.
In shorts or jeans, we take a chance,
While dodging bugs in our dance.

Old maps and snacks clutter the floor,
Who knew that we'd stop for more?
We once got lost and found a cat,
He looked at us like, 'What's up with that?'

We sing to tunes both loud and clear,
Getting lost feels like a cheer.
With coffee stains and cookie crumbs,
Our route's a game; we're all like chums.

The sun sets low, a golden glow,
Oh, what a sight as we all show.
With laughter echoing in the dark,
We choose to drive, but now we park.

Footsteps in the Moonlight

Chasing shadows, stepping light,
Underneath the stars so bright.
We trip on rocks and nearly fall,
Our giggles echo—what a call!

Navigating paths so vague,
Bumping into the friendly plague.
A raccoon steals our late-night fries,
He grins at us; what a surprise!

With moonbeams lighting our way,
We wander, dance, and laugh and play.
What's this, a trail of socks instead?
Oh wait, they're ours! Let's head to bed.

Back to the car with sleepy grins,
The moonlight waves as our fun begins.
We promise to keep next time in sight,
But for now, we'll dream of moonlit nights.

The Magic of Everyday Travels

Everyday trips become delight,
To the corner store; oh, what a sight!
We hunt for snacks, a treasure hunt,
Grabbing weird chips just for the fun.

Pedaling fast on our rusty bikes,
Making memories that everyone likes.
We race with squirrels; they take the lead,
While we laugh loud, that's all we need.

Park benches serve as our throne,
Eating ice cream, we've clearly grown.
With sticky hands and sugar highs,
No better magic under the skies.

Home again, tired yet alive,
So many stories, we must revive.
Tomorrow's journey is already planned,
With silly maps drawn in the sand.

The Quiet Beauty of Long Roads

On long roads, we whine and sing,
How much longer until we swing?
The view is nice, but wait—what's that?
A giant sign for a local cat!

Detours lead to fast food bliss,
Burgers, fries—oh, who can resist?
With crumbs on laps and windows down,
We take this road trip all around town.

Counting cars and making a list,
Shouting out every chance we missed.
Each mile adds a chuckle or two,
No frown in sight on this wild crew.

As stars appear and the night creeps in,
Roads turn quiet, where dreams begin.
We lie back, laughter fades to hums,
On quiet roads, how sweet life becomes.

Embracing the Detours

I took a turn for no good reason,
Got lost in a field of angry bees.
They buzzed like my old car's engine,
I waved, hoping they'd just let me be.

With GPS that lost its mind,
I ate snacks and danced offbeat.
A wrong way sign said 'You'll find,'
My favorite roadside BBQ treat.

My friends all laughed at my wild fate,
As I planned the craziest escape.
Who knew getting lost would create,
A legend they'll all love to drape?

Now when they ask how I explore,
I smile and say, "Oops, nevermore!"
For each wrong turn just opens a door,
To stories and treasures galore!

The Beauty of Uncharted Trails

I took a hike with mismatched shoes,
One pink, one green, quite the sight.
Tripped on roots and faced my blues,
While squirrels laughed, pure delight.

The map led me straight to a lake,
Where ducks quacked and joined my dance.
I tried to swim, what a mistake,
The water had other plans for my chance.

A snail became my travel buddy,
We climbed up a hill, oh so steep!
I sang songs, bright and muddy,
He just looked back, quite the leap!

So here's to trails without a guide,
To laughter and bumps, oh what fun!
Each step is a rollercoaster ride,
Don't forget, we're all here to run!

Whispers of the Open Road

With windows down and music loud,
I cruised past fields of cows in line.
Their moos like a curious crowd,
Clapping to my favorite design.

Red lights stopped my joyful spree,
As I closed my eyes and dreamed of fries.
A trucker waved, egging me free,
To join his parade in the skies.

I took a route that felt like fate,
An ice cream truck was on the track.
I cursed the road that made me wait,
Then got a scoop, there's no going back!

So here's to roads that twist and bend,
To laughter tucked in pockets wide.
With friends like mine, I'll never bend,
Just swerve and savor this joyride!

Serendipity on the Horizon

A flat tire on the route ahead,
I stomped my feet and said, "Oh no!"
But sunshine popped, and hope was fed,
As I found smiles everywhere I'd go.

Strangers cheered with donuts in hand,
They sang songs as I changed my wheel.
Comedy troops, they surely planned,
To turn my mishap into a reel.

A sign for gas, I turned too late,
Instead, found an art fair on the street.
Each brushstroke skipped the mundane fate,
Laughter painted my day bittersweet.

So here's to joy in unexpected bends,
And smiles that follow the loop-de-loop.
As we wander, we find true friends,
In every skip of our joyful scoop!

The Tapestry of Wandering Souls

In a car packed tight, we hit the road,
A map of memories, our playful abode.
With snacks in hand, we sing off-key,
Chasing sunsets, just you and me.

We took a wrong turn, or was it right?
Found a llama farm while driving at night.
With llamas staring, we laughed in glee,
Creating tales for our future spree.

Oh, the fast lane's not our kind of groove,
Bumping down trails, feeling the move.
With every detour, our hearts take flight,
Wandering souls, soaring with delight.

From quirky diners to the leaning trees,
Collecting moments like autumn leaves.
As we embrace the scenic fun,
Our journey has just begun.

Breathtaking Views from the Side Roads

Turn left instead of right, oh what a sight,
A giant rubber duck holds the daylight.
We had plans, but then we forgot,
And found treasures in a kooky lot.

A picnic by the creek turned into a splash,
In muddy waters, we took a dash.
With bread crumbs floating, we laughed in the sun,
Ducks quacked loudly, oh what fun!

The GPS says we're stuck in a loop,
But we're making memories, aren't we the troop?
We've seen sunflowers dancing in the breeze,
And yet to find a place that doesn't tease.

There's beauty in paths that don't lead straight,
With wobbly routes, we tempt our fate.
Each silly turn shapes our fun-filled quests,
As we gather giggles, we count our blessed.

A Symphony of Sights

Every curve whispers a playful song,
Through valleys and mountains, we don't feel wrong.
With big sun hats and shades of delight,
We dance with shadows from morning till night.

From popsicle stands to that ice cream shop,
We stumble on wonders, oh, we can't stop!
With cherry stains and cones that drip,
Laughing on corners, let's take a trip.

We'll count the trains that rattle past,
Each honk and whistle, we dream and blast.
Sights intertwine in a colorful weave,
With every laugh, our spirits believe.

Nature serenades from the winding lanes,
With breezy whispers through windowpanes.
In a world of wonders we dance and sway,
Collecting laughter along the way.

Nature's Gentle Invitations

Come step outside, where the wild things roam,
In fields of daisies, we find our home.
Bouncing off clouds, our heads in the air,
The world is a playground, with giggles to share.

We chased butterflies, they led us astray,
Past cookie-shaped rocks and a lemonade bay.
With muddy shoes and laughter so loud,
We danced with daisies, delightfully proud.

An oak tree beckons with branches so wide,
"Climb up for treasures, take a joyride!"
With toes in the stream and laughter like bells,
We savor the stories that nature compels.

So here's to the meandering paths we adore,
With love for the quirks that we can explore.
In whimsical moments, let's take a seat,
Nature's sweet laughter, a true heartbeats.

The Dance of Serendipity

Two left feet dance on winding paths,
Tripping over thoughts and grass,
A stumble here, a giggle there,
Life's odd ballet, a merry affair.

Sidewalks whisper tales untold,
Of coffee spills and ice cream molds,
Where every wrong turn's a brand new chance,
To cha-cha-cha in a clumsy dance.

With sunshine bright and clouds of gray,
I'll boogie through each quirky day,
Each twist and twirl, a punchline spun,
In this freestyle journey, oh what fun!

So grab your partner, don't be shy,
Let's salsa down the road awry,
For in this waltz of fate, you'll see,
The funny steps of serendipity.

In the Heart of the Scenic Overlook.

Up high on cliffs, where eagles dare,
I munch on snacks, without a care,
The view's a feast, but wait, oh no!
Did I drop my sandwich? What a show!

The valley's grand, like a postcard scene,
I am the queen of clumsy cuisine,
With chips in hair and crumbs on my nose,
A culinary mess, but oh how it glows!

My selfie sticks out, I'm feeling bold,
But a breeze comes by, and the story's told,
As my hat flies off, tumbling down,
I chase it like a giggling clown.

From high above, it's a playful sight,
A scenic view, yet lost in flight,
So here's to blunders, let laughter ring,
In the heart of nature, it's the joy we bring!

Winding Roads of Reflection

Curvy roads keep me on my toes,
With twists and turns, adventure grows,
I drive with snacks, the radio loud,
Blasting tunes that make me proud.

A signpost points to 'Next Left Fun',
But I miss it, and now I'm on the run,
But wait, what's that? A llama parade!
Glorious chaos, I'm glad I strayed!

Reflecting on life, I sip my drink,
In the rearview, I start to think,
Every wrong turn, a hidden gem,
With laughter as my trusty diadem.

So here I go, with no regrets,
On winding roads, the road-life bets,
In cars and laughs, let freedom flow,
It's all a ride, just enjoy the show!

Paths Less Taken

In the woods where raccoons plot,
I took the path that no one sought,
With branches swaying, a rough terrain,
Each step, a giggle, or maybe pain.

Where bushes tickle, and mud makes a mess,
I stomp like a kid, I must confess,
With every squelch, the laughter grows,
Adventure awaits, it's what I chose!

I met a squirrel that stole my snack,
He winked at me—hey, no coming back!
But all the giggles are worth the plot,
In paths less taken, I've found a lot.

So here's to trails outside the norm,
With quirks and laughs, it's in the swarm,
Just take that leap, don't hesitate,
For the best stories? They're worth the wait!

The Melody of Each Step

In slippers worn and laces tied,
I dance through puddles, let giggles ride.
The pavement sings beneath my feet,
As I shuffle along, a silly beat.

I twirl past squirrels in a frantic race,
They mock my moves with a fuzzy face.
Each hop and skip, I add a flair,
The sidewalk's stage is my best affair.

The wind throws laughter, a playful tease,
My hat takes flight like a paper breeze.
"Oh no!" I shout, as I chase it back,
My feet keep dancing, no time to slack.

With every step, my worries dissolve,
In the rhythmic chaos, I find resolve.
Life's a jig, come join the fun,
With every misstep, we truly run.

The Essence of the Road Unseen

An empty street, I wander wide,
With mystery as my trusty guide.
Pavement cracks, like stories told,
In every bump, a treasure, bold.

I find a cat with a fancy hat,
He's the king, and I'm his brat.
We stroll together, quite the pair,
In this upside-down affair we share.

A twisty path with unexpected bends,
Where even the trees are quirky friends.
I giggle at the bushes dressed in green,
Their secret whispers, a playful scene.

Each twist reveals a plot unique,
Every corner hides a cheeky peek.
And as I wander, joy's my plea,
The road unseen sets my spirit free.

Dreaming at Every Crossroad

Two paths diverge, oh what to do?
Each one shines like a bright debut.
I flip a coin, it starts to spin,
Life's just a gamble; let the fun begin!

One path looks serious, dressed in gray,
The other boasts colors, come out to play!
I choose the latter, worn-out shoes,
With hiccups of joy and possible snooze.

A signpost wiggles, it whispers loud,
"Take the long way!"—it draws a crowd.
Traffic jams of laughter and glee,
I follow the nonsense, it's where I want to be.

So dream at each crossroad, flummoxed and free,
With absurd options, just let it be!
A twist here, a honk there, in playful delight,
I'll wander this maze until it feels right.

Paintbrushes of the Skies

The sunset spills like spilled paint,
A masterpiece, though slightly quaint.
Brush strokes twirl and colors clash,
It's like a canvas caught in a splash!

Clouds wear hats, quite the charade,
As if the sky's in a silly parade.
A sunbeam tickles, bursts in cheer,
It wraps me up, says, "Don't you fear!"

With every giggle, I chase the rays,
And dance with shadows in a goofy haze.
The world's a gallery, so bright and wide,
With paintbrushes swirling in every stride.

So let's dip our toes in these waters bold,
And color our hearts with laughter untold.
With skies as our canvas, let's play and fly,
In the art of being, we'll simply get by.

Fleeting Glimpses of Joy

Every corner hides a surprise,
A squirrel with a nut, oh my!
We laugh at the chickens on parade,
Chasing dreams in a lemonade shade.

The road is long, let's not be shy,
With funky hats, we'll wave goodbye.
Puddles splashed, socks soaking wet,
Wishing for joy, we're the best duet.

Secrets Beneath the Sky

Clouds dance around like silly clowns,
A kite gets tangled, oh how it frowns!
Invisible maps lead us astray,
But ice cream cones save the day.

With every step, there's laughter loud,
Like insects screaming, "We're so proud!"
There's joy in whispers, secrets we trade,
Beneath the stars where plans are laid.

Traveling Souls

Two friends on bikes, what a sight,
Pedaling fast in the evening light.
The world's a stage, each stop a scene,
A muddy bump, oh what a sheen!

We trade our snacks as if they're gold,
With spicy chips, our stories unfold.
A journey painted with giggles and cheer,
In a world where happiness is near.

Shared Stories

On this road, tales bounce like balls,
From epic fails to weird cat calls.
A talking tree with a fancy hat,
It tells us jokes about a flying rat.

We scribble laughs in the dust of the road,
And share more secrets than our hearts hold.
With each little trip, memories reside,
In this wacky vehicle we call pride.

Where the Wild Things Roam

In a land where giggles bloom like flowers,
Wild things roam for hours and hours.
With marshmallow clouds and jellybean trees,
We find joy in a sneaky breeze.

The map is twisted, the rules are bent,
Our hearts are light, our souls content.
Let's dance with shadows, spin with fate,
In this adventure, we celebrate!

Visions of Tomorrow's Wander

With a map upside down, I start on my quest,
All my friends laugh, say it's for the best.
Each step that I take leads me far from my goal,
But hey, there's a donut shop on this stroll!

Found a treasure trove of snacks on the way,
I was seeking adventure, but muffins will stay.
Wanderlust wound up tangled in crumbs,
This scenic route, oh, how it hums!

Horizons of Hope and Beyond

I packed all my dreams in a suitcase so bright,
But forgot to check if it zipped up tight.
Now my hopes are spilling all over the floor,
Looks like I'm destined to dream even more!

Through valleys of laughter and mountains of cheese,
I stumble on wisdom in soft, sticky fees.
Maybe I'll find fortune in ridiculous schemes,
Or just a good nap, wrapped in my dreams!

Paths of Light

Stumbled through shadows, where giggles reside,
With squirrels as my guides, and my cat purring wide.
Each path takes a twist, like a corndog on a stick,
Why walk straight ahead? Let's do a cool trick!

Under the stars, I dance with a chair,
Even lost my shoes—oh, what a great scare!
Yet laughter lights paths in the darkening night,
And I'll keep on wandering till morning feels right!

Roads of Shadows

In the land of forgotten and shadowy bends,
I laugh at the bends with my most foolish friends.
While searching for wisdom, we found potato chips,
And an alarming amount of pickle-flavored dips!

Each corner I turn feels like a taco surprise,
But they always lead back to my bright, hungry eyes.
Let's take the long route, it's safer—I'm told,
Unless you count all of the secrets we fold!

Remnants of the Lost Traveler

Once I traveled light with a bag full of snacks,
But the trail turned into a quest for more Slack.
Between fast-food dumpsters and questing for fries,
I found the real treasure, a drumstick disguise.

Lessons I learned from the mishaps galore,
Like when to stop wandering and just hit the store.
But each little stumble, though goofy and wild,
Turns out to be part of the trip, not just mild!

Collecting Memories in a Dusty Journal

I tried to write it down, my day so bright,
But every page's blank, oh what a sight.
A cat walked by, I tripped on a shoe,
Now I'm scribbling 'whoops'—my best debut.

Got lost in a maze of mismatched socks,
Torn between the beach and a box of rocks.
A scoop of ice cream, oh, what a delight,
But then I dropped it—was that a seagull in flight?

Old photos remind me of parties and pranks,
Where I danced with a broom, filled in the blanks.
Each spill and each thrill, they bring me such glee,
This dust-covered journal, it's a treasure to me.

So if you find me with a grin ear to ear,
Just know I'm collecting the things I hold dear.
With each quirky tale turning pages that twirl,
My life's one big giggle—like cats on a whirl.

Beyond the Straight and Narrow

They told me to stick to the well-paved way,
But who needs directions on such a fine day?
I took a left turn, then right at the tree,
Ran into my neighbor—plastered with brie.

My GPS yelled, 'Recalculating route!'
I just laughed at my luck, feeling rather astute.
Found a dance party in the town's old square,
With disco balls and folks in wild hair!

Chased a squirrel thinking it had all the clues,
What a mistake—now it's gone with my shoes!
Yet every misstep leads to fun, not a frown,
Just a whimsical tale in this topsy-turvy town.

Beyond straight lanes where rules often bind,
There's adventure and laughter, a fun state of mind.
So here's to errors and zigzagged paths,
For that's where we find all our goofy big laughs.

The Art of Getting Lost

I set off to work, coffee in hand,
But somehow forgot—what a goof, isn't it grand?
Stumbled on a market with treats piled high,
Now I'm a happy mess with pie in my eye.

Maps are for sailors—I've my own secret code,
Just follow the smells wherever I strode.
A detour through laughter and giggles galore,
Surprises await me, who could ask for more?

I ended at a party dressed as a cow,
What started as chaos? I don't know how!
But mooing and dancing soaked up the hot sun,
Lost in the joy, I've already won.

So here's to the paths that twist and they twine,
Every misstep I take tastes like good wine.
Getting lost is the art I've perfectly found,
In the silly and strange, joy's profoundly unbound.

Shimmering Horizons

Chasing sunsets on a bicycle ride,
The wind in my hair, my friend by my side.
But in my excitement, I took the wrong track,
Now we're on a trail with ducks—what a quack!

We laughed at the skies, reds and oranges ablaze,
Who needs a map in this whimsical maze?
Each twist and each turn brings a chuckle and spin,
With horizons that shimmer, let's go dive in!

Found a turtle crossing, thought it was grand,
He took his sweet time, didn't care where we planned.
With a wink, I whispered, "You're wise, oh so slow,"
He blinked back at me as if saying, 'Let's go.'

So pedal on forward, with hearts full of cheer,
In this crazy adventure, the end isn't near.
With shimmering horizons wrapped wide in the glow,
Each giggle and smile is the wild card we show.

www.ingramcontent.com/pod-product-compliance
Lightning Source LLC
Chambersburg PA
CBHW071848160426
43209CB00003B/468